Heart of the Headland

When Hilda came to Hartlepool

Elisabeth Westhead

MAPLE
PUBLISHERS

Heart of the Headland

Author: Elisabeth Westhead

Copyright © Elisabeth Westhead (2025)

The right of Elisabeth Westhead to be identified as author of this work has been asserted by the author in accordance with section 77 and 78 of the Copyright, Designs and Patents Act 1988.

First Published in 2025

ISBN 978-1-83538-597-5 (Paperback)
      978-1-83538-598-2 (E-Book)

Book Cover, Illustrations and Layout by:
    White Magic Studios
    www.whitemagicstudios.co.uk

Published by:
    Maple Publishers
    Fairbourne Drive, Atterbury,
    Milton Keynes,
    MK10 9RG, UK
    www.maplepublishers.com

A CIP catalogue record for this title is available from the British Library.
All rights reserved. No part of this book may be reproduced or translated by any form or by any means, electronic or mechanical, including photocopying, recording or by any information storage and retrieval system without written permission from the author.

Contents

FOREWORD 5
PREFACE 9
FINDING THE FIRST NAMESTONE 14

Chapter 1
    THE CHRISTIAN MISSIONARIES 18

Chapter 2
    THE SAINTS 27

Chapter 3
    THE VENERABLE BEDE 37

Chapter 4
    ABBESS HILDA 41

Chapter 5
    THE SYNOD OF WHITBY. AD 664 49

Chapter 6
    ARCHAEOLOGY 54

Chapter 7
    THE PORT 61

Contents

Chapter 8
    THE FRIARY 67

Chapter 9
    ARCHITECTURE 69

Chapter 10
    NAME-DROPPING A TOUR INSIDE THE CHURCH 79

Chapter 11
    PILGRIMAGE ROUTES 90

Chapter 12
    THE ROLE OF THE CHURCH IN THE TWENTY-FIRST CENTURY 94

CONCLUSION 100

BIBLIOGRAPHY 103

MY THANKS 104

APPENDIX
    Detailing: STAINED GLASS WINDOWS, ARCHITECTS and ORGAN 106

FOREWORD

Guidebooks for churches are often a bit dull, frankly. Sorry, but that is what I find. They frequently go into excessive detail about the exact date that a new porch was added (or fell over) or who all the vicars were. Whether their sermons were life-changing or min-numbingly boring, and their example inspiring or deeply disappointing, we get the full list of their dates anyway!

Elisabeth Westhead has given St Hilda's a much better gift than that in this booklet!

She explains the place of St Hilda's church in the history of Christianity in our region, in a way that really helps us imagine the very different lives that people who were otherwise very like us lived. This history includes the relationship of this church to the Christian leader we call St Hilda, who lived, worked and cared for people in this place centuries before the church that bears her name came to be built.

St Hilda's is a hugely important building in heritage terms. Elisabeth explains how, in spite of this, it has known times when it fell into disrepair and needed substantial funds and serious work to restore it. That challenge remains: local churches are exactly that, and – contrary to the popular belief that they receive support from the government or the Church of England centrally (they don't) – they are maintained and managed by local people. It is often a fairly small number of local people, those who make the commitment to be part of the worshipping community and give regularly. They don't often get much recognition and thanks for that (so, thank you, everyone at St Hilda's). At times, some additional resources really are needed. Elisabeth tells us the history of such investments in the past, and she does so at a time when St Hilda's is currently receiving a substantial sum from the Heritage Lottery Fund to both restore this beautiful place and open it to the community it is here to serve.

It is good that this this grant has been made, because St Hilda's is indeed an important heritage building. This is partly a matter of architecture and antiquity, of course. However, like all ancient churches, St Hilda's is only here at all (and has only remained) because people believed that faith in Jesus Christ is so important that it needs spaces like this. They believed that there should be fine buildings, like this one, which speak by their very form of the beauty and love of God, where that God may discovered in every generation, worshipped, and bring people together as a community with faith at their centre. A church unmoored from that vision and purpose can at best become a museum, like a fine country house no longer lived in but preserved for posterity, and experienced only as a tourist attraction.

Elisabeth is clear that the church which bears St Hilda's name is a church – a place where the love of God is celebrated and shared. She writes in chapter 9:

'It is visible from the sea and all around, and represents a symbol of the Christian faith dating back into history and carrying forward the responsibility for all its history, hopefully into a new future of hope and certainty.'

She also writes with openness and real humility about what that future may be, in the middle of times of great need, fear and uncertainty (and indeed anger) in the town St Hilda's is here to serve. How shall the church offer hope, love and joy today?

That future, and that ongoing mission, do need the extra resources currently being received to restore and reorder the church building, and we are thankful for that. But it will also always need – at its core and as its beating heart – a community of women, men and children who find hope, love and joy themselves in the life and worship of the church. What they find they can then share. It is in that sharing of God's love in many ways, with the church building as a resource and a spiritual home, that the church body continues the tradition of Hilda. (Also, unless this church community thrives, there will be no one here in generations to come to love this church building and secure its future for the purpose it was built.)

Elisabeth's booklet raises these questions for the future by rooting us in the past. We get a good and lively history lesson, but one which asks us to imagine with hope how the chapters of the history of St Hilda's church as yet unwritten may unfold – and how they may tell a story of good news, in every way.

The Venerable Rick Simpson

Archdeacon of Auckland

January 2025

PREFACE

I write about St Hilda's church on Hartlepool Headland as a relative newcomer to the area, although I did have ancestors who lived on the Headland for nearly 100 years. And when I was aged two, my mother, Hilda, brought me to visit my great great aunts Hilda and Margaret in Catherine Street. My ancestors came from Lerwick for the shipping boom, then left as the industry declined, with my aunts staying on as teachers. The Headland was always prone to these booms in prosperity. It's my belief that the greatest times for the Headland and its church were long ago in Anglo Saxon times when the Celtic saints came as missionaries and Hartlepool was at the forefront of the shaping of English Christianity. St Hilda's church is probably unique because of its connections with Lindisfarne and St Aidan. Archaeological findings suggest that Whitby Abbey, even under St Hilda, was much more under the influence of Rome and European culture. Now I live here, I do have a personal association with this part of the world, and now I am privileged to be able to attend the Headland and this lovely church every week.

Elisabeth Westhead

I think the most important history of the Hartlepool Headland and St Hilda has been forgotten and overlooked. I lived in Whitby at the bottom of the 199 steps, just below the Abbey, for 11 years and I was inspired by St Hilda. Now I live in Hartlepool and attend church on St Hilda's earlier site. I want to share that inspiration, and show the depth and power of the history that still lingers on the Headland. In this booklet I want to give an overview, and look at the church in different ways - its site, the inspiration that created the church in the first place, the stories and legends that surround it, and its importance in the community today in the twenty-first century. My theme is to promote St Hilda's church through the ages, and make out a case for it being much more significant in British Christian history than it is given credit for. I need to ignore some lesser and much loved historical details to bring to the fore events in Northumbria which helped shape Christianity in Britain, and in consequence the formation of the country we are to day. My hope is to bring together the stories the hopes and aspirations, in a wide network, showing how they make St. Hilda's church a beloved place of worship and a landmark into the future.

Nikolaus Pevsner in 'The Buildings of England' calls St. Hilda's :

Heart of the Headland

'One of the most important churches in the county'. And Martin Roberts in 'The New Pevsner Guide' writes of the Headland: 'One of the most important historic landscapes in the county, medieval walls against a little beach, colourful Georgian grandeur, dockside cranes, oil platforms and shipping'. The National Churches Trust rates it as one of the most important churches in the North of England. This 800-year-old church in the centre of it all with its beautiful cathedral-like interior, connects so many stories, historical figures, legends, pathways all set on an ancient holy site. It really merits more than a booklet - but this is just my attempt to weave together all the threads to make as grand piece of cloth, as I can.

I am dealing with Hartlepool Headland, from the beginning to the present in approximately chronological order, starting with Bishop Paulinus, sent North from Kent, and Bishop Aidan who left Iona to convert the people of the North of England, then St Hilda - the heroine of our story - because she inspired everything that followed. Without Bede, the historian, we probably would not know who they were, and all their stories. It was he who brought all these saints alive for us so we can almost feel we knew them. The seventh century was a most unsettled time, when Germanic tribes were arriving from Europe and fighting over land boundaries. As for Hartlepool, it was Bishop Aidan, the Venerable Bede and Abbess Hilda, in all their different ways who dedicated their lives to the hope that Christianity would bring their communities back together to work in harmony and peace.

In a few short pages I skim over fourteen centuries. It is the people more than the events that inspire, and just for a short time in the North East of England, the the Celtic church with its Irish culture, was dominant here with its leaders, Oswald, Aidan, Hilda and Cuthbert and historian Bede telling us all about what was going on. Our Celtic Anglo-Saxon saints are of vital importance to this area and this church. Despite the historical remoteness, their characters are still alive, and their influence still felt by many, and their portraits are glowing in our stained glass windows.

As you look at St. Hilda's on the Headland, you are bound to wonder why such a large and beautiful structure should be put on this rather isolated site. Is it simply a place for people to go and worship? Has it a special significance? What has happened on this peninsular/island in the past? What inspired the architects and the builders? How has the population been able to afford its maintenance over 800 years of history? How much is it loved? What historical figures, if any, have been involved in its history? And - the most pressing question of all

Heart of the Headland

- how will Hartlepudlians find the will and inspiration to continue to worship there and preserve it for the next 800 years?

I hope to bring out its significance. I want to show how it was inspired by missionaries, and then Celtic Christians, its connections to royalty, its involvement in the formation of Christianity in the UK, how it continues to inspire artists and musicians and seamen, and is in the twenty-first century, the starting place for pilgrimages.

It would be fitting for it to be seen as a special place of beauty and Christian inspiration for the next 800 years. As the Venerable Bede wanted his writing to incentivise and bring together the peoples of England in the 'Dark Ages', and as Abbess Hilda brought together rival factions at the Synod of Whitby, we hope the church of St. Hilda in Hartlepool, can remain the Heart of the Headland, and stand as a Beacon of Hope in the next few centuries.

Elisabeth Westhead

FINDING THE FIRST NAMESTONE

"In the month of July last, in digging the foundations of a house belonging to Mr John Bulmer, in a field called 'Cross Close' at a distance of about 135 yards from the present church-yard in a south-easterly direction, at the depth of three feet and a half, and immediately upon the limestone, the workmen discovered several skeletons lying in a position nearly north and south. The bones were carefully removed under the superintendance of Mr Bulmer and Mr Eeles, and deposited in the church-yard.

A large number of the skulls were resting on small flat plain stones, varying from four to five inches square, and under a few were discovered stones bearing inscriptions, and marked with the cross. ....

(That) the inscriptions ..... are ancient and evidently Runic....does not admit of a doubt.....

On the 'reading' of the inscriptions, however, much will depend, and I therefore spare you'll further speculations for the present."

Extracts from the Gentleman's Magazine for September 1833, page 219.

"As all proper names indicate a quality of mind or body, reputed excellent by our forefathers, we are doubtful whether the second word denotes a proper name, or an epithet containing the encomium of the deceased. I deem the latter most probable."

Comment from Mr Bosworth, author of the AngloSaxon Dictionary. Feb 1886

Elisabeth Westhead

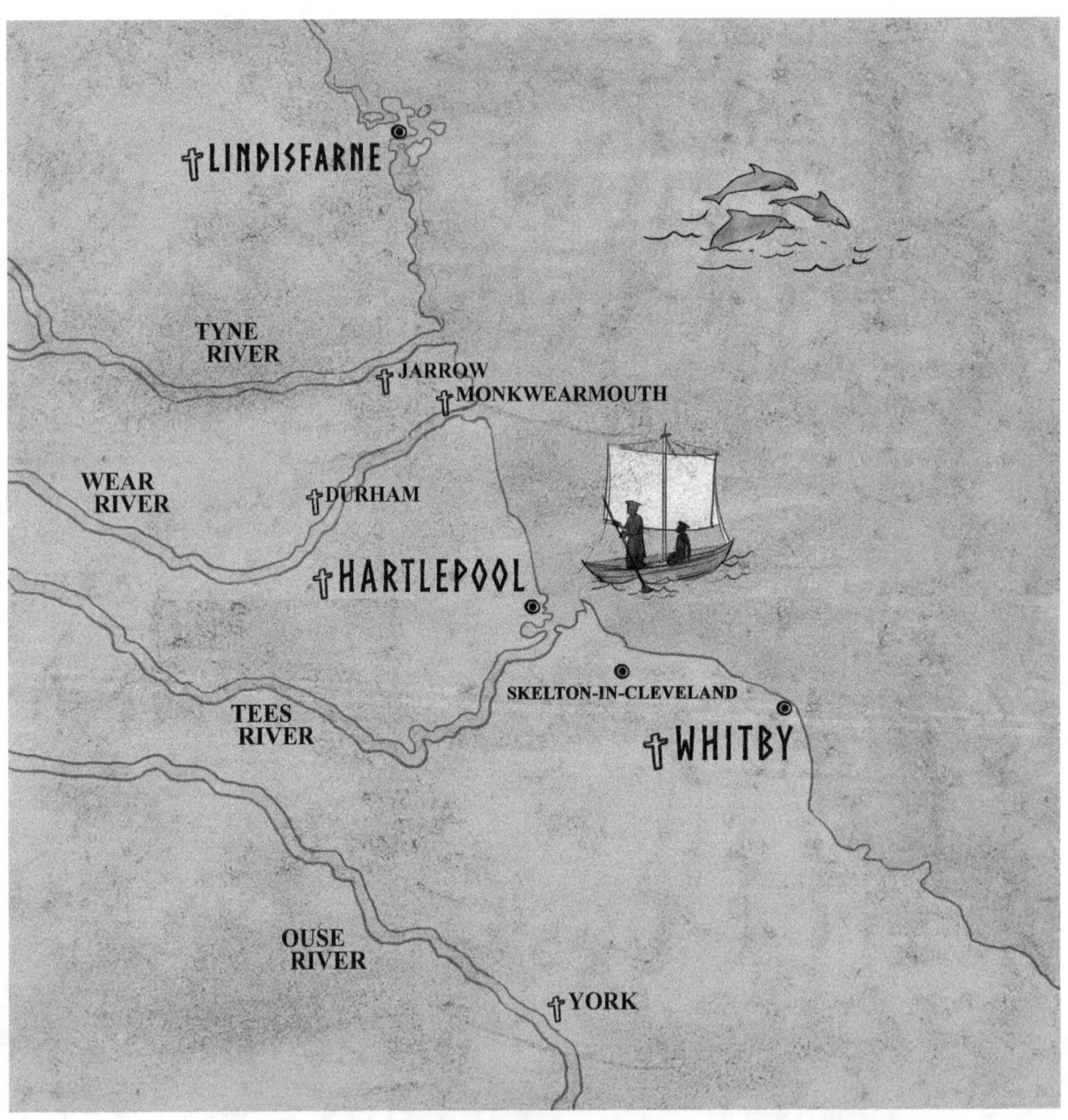

Chapter 1
THE CHRISTIAN MISSIONARIES

There have been more than 36 archaeological excavations on Hartlepool Headland during the last two centuries. There cannot be many other villages in the UK that can boast of so much attention. There is little chance of uncovering hoards of gold here. Instead, historians are excited to find the traces of a seventh century monastery, inspired by Irish missionaries. St Hilda came here around 647 AD as Abbess of this new monastery. She became a powerful and much loved figure in an age dominated by men. The archaeology of this unique place has revealed a great deal about Anglo-Saxon life and the roots of early Christianity as it was lived on this remote little headland. My book is an attempt to show how ancient history is reflected through the centuries and how it impacts the twenty-first century.

Our church of St Hilda is not just a stone structure. It represents very early triumphs and struggles in the emergence of Christianity in England.

Heart of the Headland

The North Eastern saints in particular are treasured. Because they brought their Christianity to this region, because Bede wrote about them, often with first hand knowledge, and brought them to life. We feel almost that they are people we know personally. It was not just Hilda whose voice echoes down the ages, also Aidan who sent her, Oswald who summoned Aidan, and popular Cuthbert. These were Celtic saints and they were called 'saints' because the people loved them and they were perceived to have performed miracles. In Anglo-Saxon times, things were more fluid, and there was no bureaucracy to rubber-stamp them as 'saints'. They were loved and revered by their followers, and some of that emotion still persists down the ages.

So most of this book is looking at the effects of that ancient history. It is an attempt to show what inspired our beautiful church and what lies underneath it. The roots of my story inevitably go back a long, long way, seeing as I want to show how Roman missionaries and Irish missionaries arrived together, in Anglo-Saxon times, and clashed.

Christianity had first come to England during the Roman occupation. Emperor Constantine had made it the state religion in the fourth century. But the Romans left after four centuries, and pagans from Germanic countries had invaded. This book begins with the Venerable

Elisabeth Westhead

Bede in Jarrow, on the River Tyne, King Oswald of Northumberland, and Pope Gregory in Rome who were all concerned to bring the faith, and with it, peace, to the North of this now 'barbarian' island.

By the seventh century, which is where our story starts, the world was in turmoil. Different styles of Christianity were emerging. Hartlepool and the North East of England had a big part to play in the introduction of Christianity to England. It was the Celtic brand that arrived on Hartlepool Headland with the Celtic saints and St Hilda. And it was their arrival which makes the history of the Headland so unique.

Pope Gregory, far away in Rome, was keen to make an impression and rebuild the power of the popes in Rome after the capital had been ruined by the Visigoth invasion. Had the Visigoths not sacked Rome, then Celtic Christianity might have persisted longer in Britain, and the Synod of Whitby might have happened much later than it did. As it was, the Pope saw Britannia being invaded by Germanic pagans, and rapidly reverting to paganism. And as Pope in Rome, he felt threatened by the Celtic branch of Christianity, so he sent Augustine to Kent in AD 597. This was the first outreach from the Catholic Church. It happened a long way from Bernicia, but it had a knock-on effect.

Heart of the Headland

Back in the year 600 AD, the kingdoms of Bernicia (Northumberland) and Deira (Yorkshire) would follow a pattern - like St Hilda herself - first pagan, then Celtic Christian, and after the Synod of Whitby, the Northern Royal Family would be under the influence of Rome. For a short time on the Headland, and in Northumbria, it was Celtic Christianity from Ireland, that dominated. In this book I am trying to look at that era in more detail, and show how it still influences life fourteen centuries later.

When pagan King Edwin of Northumbria wanted to marry Aethelburga, daughter of the Kentish king, her father would only allow the marriage if Edwin became a Christian. Edwin agreed to this, and Queen Aethelburga came north with Bishop Paulinus to introduce the faith (Roman Christianity) in Northumbria. In AD 627, he baptised some members of Northern Royalty including St Hilda in York. (Then he built a wooden church there, and this would represent the earliest beginnings of the archbishopric of York, now part of the structure of the Church of England.)

The newly Christianised King Edwin, however, died young in battle. Paulinus was forgotten for the time being. Oswald, became the new King of Northumbria, and he fancied a different way of introducing Christianity to his kingdom, and sent to Ireland for an alternative sort of bishop, an Irish Celtic bishop. As a result Irish St Aidan came from Iona with a group of monks as a missionary to Northumbria.

ST AIDAN

St Aidan arrived after Paulinus' visit, in AD 635. He was an Irish speaker, sent from the island of Iona, off the West coast of Scotland, bringing a number of Iona monks with him. Bede describes him as *'a man of outstanding gentleness, holiness and moderation, who is much respected'*. Considering that he had to learn Anglo-Saxon before he could go preaching, Aidan was remarkably successful in his mission. For 30 years, maybe even half a century, in Northumbria, Celtic culture was the rule.

With his monks, he probably walked through Glen Coe and then followed one of the Roman border walls - Antonine or Hadrian's- to reach the North East coast, and then King Oswald gave him land so they could set up a monastery on the island of Lindisfarne.

Heart of the Headland

Lindisfarne is cut off from the mainland by the tides every day. It was the sort of place that the Celts liked and chose for their monasteries, and the monks continued to flourish and feel safe there until Viking Raids ultimately drove them away in AD 793. Just as Columba had chosen to settle and make his community on the island of Iona, Aidan concentrated on building his Abbey on the little island of Lindisfarne. Hartlepool Headland, is a 100 miles south, standing on a ridge of hard white Magnesian limestone which may have once been an island when the sands around it washed away. It looked to Aidan like a good place for Hilda to set up her monastery.

Bede writes in his history that Aidan preferred to walk everywhere and he says that every time Aidan met people on his walks he would stop and talk with them. (By this time he had probably learned to speak Anglo-Saxon!) Legend has it that the King gave Aidan a horse to make his missionary work easier and that Aidan - because he enjoyed walking - gave the horse away to a beggar, who seemed more need of it than he did. Being Irish, and promoting Celtic Christianity he loved the simple ways and avoided pomp. This story demonstrates how Celtic culture was different from Roman ways.

In order to imagine how this Headland settlement was organised, we need to understand how the Celtic monasteries reflected the Irish lifestyle.

Elisabeth Westhead

In Ireland at this time, with no towns and no proper roads, (unlike the structured Roman culture of Pope Gregory, Augustine and Paulinus), the Celtic style monasteries that they set up in Northern England, were more like big villages than the later monasteries. There will have been a few hermits and a few priests at the centre of the community, but research shows that in these early monasteries there were married couples living on the fringes as well, and they were all called 'monks', both men and women. Some historians think that St Hilda herself was already married and had children even before she was made Abbess. The cemeteries excavated on the Headland contain skeletons of children, as well as the older nuns and monks that we would expect to find buried there. The monasteries in both Hartlepool and at first, Whitby, followed the Celtic tradition, and so were like villages celebrating Christianity. Later Roman Style monasteries, like Rievaulx, near Helmsley in Yorkshire, were single sex with an austere regime.

Irish missionaries, like Aidan and his monks, travelled on foot, and were hardy. They are often pictured wearing long cloaks against rain and wind, carrying tall poles to manage the rough terrain, and a bell to summon their listeners. Aidan is depicted this way in stained glass windows and pictures.

Heart of the Headland

To us, Lindisfarne seems a remote place from which to convert the population of Northumbria, until we understand that most communications were made by boat. We tend to think of medieval Irish people rowing coracles about on Irish lakes. Yet it is almost certain that they knew how to sail, and could easily travel from Lindisfarne to Jarrow, and Jarrow to Hartlepool, along the North Sea coast.

It was St Aidan, who some twenty years after his arrival, located St Hilda, who was in East Anglia with her uncle, at the time, and he called her first to train in Wearmouth (Sunderland) and then to be abbess in Hartlepool. Royal figures like Hilda would be put in charge of communities, and it was expected that the monasteries themselves would demonstrate a better way of life, with the advantages of education, and Christianity would be spread this way, trickling down from the richest in the land to the commoners.

Once Abbess Hilda had settled in Hartlepool, Aidan would visit regularly to instruct her and help her in her new duties. So Aidan actually visited Hartlepool Headland, tying up at the nearby quayside and walking along the path where there is now a little park, through the land that Aidan gave to Abbess Heiu and then Abbess Hilda to develop. We know in so much detail about these people, because Bede had first-hand knowledge and wrote so clearly and thoughtfully. And then because many teams of archaeologists have visited to uncover our rich history.

Irish Aidan, became bishop of Lindisfarne in AD 635, and died in Bamburgh in AD 651. Bede praises him, saying how the: 'course of his life was so different from the slothfulness of our times'. He is today celebrated as the patron saint of firefighters, because he prayed successfully for the town of Bamburgh when pagans set it on fire.

Chapter 2
THE SAINTS

Anglo-Saxon Saints were much more like our modern celebrities than the canonised saints of the 21st century. Canonisation is a modern and bureaucratic process, which takes years to complete. These early saints were given their status by the recognition of the people. Bede takes care to associate each saint with a miracle or two, because it was the miracles that justified them being made saints in the first place. They were usually of royal blood. They became popular because of the charitable deeds that they did, and they were known for the miracles they performed. Even after death, their bodies were still considered to be capable of healing and doing miracles. So for centuries after Cuthbert's death, pilgrims flocked to his tomb in Durham Cathedral. Just as St Thomas a Becket's followers streamed to Canterbury, all in the hope of a cure.

St Hilda's church, built as it is on the site of Hilda's monastery, has a very special relationship with the Anglo-Saxon Christians. Instead of just being told 'stories of the saints' from some church pamphlet or other, with help from Bede, the congregation of this church almost has a personal connection with these ancient people, who walked on their land and educated the commoners in a peaceful way of life, and buried their dead in the soil, where there are now gardens, and where the tourists walk.

British people today are still superstitious, perhaps less about miracles and relics, and more about football matches or lottery wins. Just in different ways from their Anglo-Saxon ancestors. Human nature has not changed so much in the intervening centuries. I want to tell the stories here of St Bega (Abbess Heiu) and King Oswald because they also have a significant part to play in the history of St Hilda's Church on Hartlepool Headland. They are each paired with miracles, as that was what gave them the right to be called saints. Then there is a short section about St Cuthbert, because he is much loved in the region and I could not think to leave him out.

ST BEGA

The Abbess that Bede called 'Heiu' is assumed to be St Bega. She was an Irish Princess who escaped from her home country to Northern England because her father had arranged for her to marry a Viking prince, and she was not keen on this idea. Wanting to keep her

Heart of the Headland

virginity intact, she ran away. After crossing the Irish Sea, she made her life as an anchoress in a remote part of Cumbria for many years, then came to Hartlepool briefly to be the first female Abbess in England. Bega only stayed a short time in Hartlepool, then left for Tadcaster.

Her best known miracle was for the monks who came to her asking her to tell them about the boundaries of their monastery lands, and then when the snow fell, covering the land all around, but leaving untouched the area round the monastery, this was considered to be the miraculous answer to their query. Her feast day is celebrated in the town of St Bees every year, and a walk has been developed in her name taking in St Bees and Bassenthwaite in a figure of eight shape. When she moved to Northumbria, she left her only possession of worth, a bracelet, with the people of Cumbria. She is thought to have died in AD 681.

ST OSWALD

Oswald, the nephew of King Edwin, was spending time in Scotland when his Uncle died, and so he came South to claim the throne of Bernicia. After a troubled couple of years, he managed to unite the warring kingdoms of Benicia and its neighbour Deira. This made him overlord of a huge kingdom stretching almost from Edinburgh to Hull. He used Christianity as a tool in bringing people together.

He brought peace to this big kingdom, and involved himself in good works. He gained a reputation for healing people. Influenced by his time in Scotland, he favoured the Celtic strain of Christianity. So it was Oswald who requested Aidan to come as a missionary from Iona to bring Celtic Christianity to Northumbria.

During his reign, invited to a feast one day, St Aidan blessed King Oswald's hand, citing how Oswald used this hand in all the good works that he did for the poor. It was a short reign - only about ten years - before the King died in battle fighting against Penda, the pagan king of Mercia, in AD 642. He was dismembered by his enemies. Northumbrians clamoured to be given body pieces to cherish as relics but the hand blessed by Aidan was the most popular of all the relics.

That hand was important because it had been blessed by St

Heart of the Headland

Aidan, but the other body parts were also in demand. His head caused controversy, because it was considered a pagan custom (and not Christian) to venerate heads, and since his followers were Christian they did not want to be caught following pagan customs, even though they venerated the other body parts. Confusingly, there were claims all over Europe, from the Netherlands and Switzerland and elsewhere that each country had possession of his severed head. I have found two different accounts of what finally happened to the head. One claimed it was put in Cuthbert's coffin and kept in Durham Cathedral. The other said his head had come to rest in York Minster. The maker of stained-glass windows in St Hilda's church in Hartlepool, obviously thought the head was in Cuthbert's coffin.

Every now and then history gives us hints , showing the different systems of belief that were to be found running parallel in the seventh century. There were pagan rituals brought by recent settlers from Germany, Irish Christianity brought by the Celtic monks to Lindisfarne and the North, old Roman Christianity left by Constantine and the departed Romans, and a more confident Roman Christianity brought by Augustine from Pope Gregory in Rome.

Bede- through his writing, Oswald- in bringing Aidan, King Oswy- by calling the Synod of Whitby, were in their different ways, all profiting from the new Christianity, working to bring peace and coherence to the North.

These Anglo-Saxon Kings and their Bishops used their skills and influence bringing together this vast area, from the Firth of Forth, down to the Humber, while also doing their bit in the shaping of Christianity in the land. Their achievements were significant and would resound through the ages. It is my opinion that our big church on Hartlepool Headland, standing for eight hundred years on the top of the ridge, surrounded by the North Sea on three sides, carries the echoes from all those years ago deep in its stones. And the little cemetery plots where the monks and the nuns were buried on the Headland, continue to remind us of the secrets of Lindisfarne and St Hilda after all the centuries that have passed.

ST CUTHBERT

Lindisfarne Abbey made connections, later on, not just with Hilda's Abbey in the south of Bernicia, but also with Melrose in the North. Hence there came a time when the Abbot of Melrose Abbey was in charge of Lindisfarne as well. It was here in the Borders that Cuthbert was educated, on the River Tweed, in the mid seventh century. We know he visited Whitby Abbey, as there is a beautiful

Heart of the Headland

illustration of him demonstrating his healing power with Abbess Aelfflaed, Hilda's successor. He links Lindisfarne with Durham, where Durham Cathedral continues to be in charge of Hartlepool churches to this day.

Cuthbert, the monk, left Melrose Abbey as an adult, and moved to the Farne Islands. Renowned for healing and miracles, the people loved him. He was also a skilful speaker and his eyes sparkled as he preached. For a time, Cuthbert chose to live uncomfortably, perched, as a hermit, on the edge of the Inner Farne Island. Like the most revered of the saints he withdrew from ordinary life to live in difficult circumstances to punish the body and fight his inner demons. This sort of asceticism could be compared to what top athletes put themselves through today, and they were admired for it. Nowadays these islands are protected bird sanctuaries, and Cuthbert loved birds, choosing to make his home among them, and he even created a law to protect the ducks - Cuddy ducks. There exists a story, however, that he publicly shot two

ravens, symbolically showing how he renounced the paganism of Germanic Odin in order to embrace Christianity. In the end, he found his little island an increasingly uncomfortable place to live, with little protection from the North Sea, its winter storms and hurricanes.

His last few years were spent on Lindisfarne in the monastery, and he was consecrated Bishop there for the last two years of his life, AD 685-687.

Despite the fact that he had requested they bury him on his favourite Inner Farne Island he was eventually persuaded to let the monks inter him in the church on Lindisfarne where he remained, until the Vikings (Scandinavians) started raiding the East Coast. The Angles, Jutes and Saxons had arrived on our coasts without creating too much upheaval, unlike the Vikings who chose to create fear. In AD 793 or thereabouts, there was a serious threat from the raiding Vikings, and as the monks of Lindisfarne did not want to leave the body of such a beloved bishop to Viking destruction, they dug him up, and carried the body, in his elaborate coffin, around the Tyne /Wear area for a century or so, looking for a suitable site to re-bury him. Finally they arrived at that happy loop in the river Wear, which we now call Durham. Legend had it that the monks were fated to carry Cuthbert's coffin around until they found a dun cow. It makes more

Heart of the Headland

sense to believe that they chose the site to build a great cathedral that was safe and easily defended, where he could be deposited securely in the crypt with this massive Norman cathedral built all around him.

The pectoral cross found with him, symbolises both the warrior class, with its pattern of gold and garnets, and the new Christian religion by its cruciform shape His elaborately carved coffin is the oldest piece of decorated wooden carving to survive from Anglo-Saxon England. Along one side are carvings of archangels, which were supposedly a throwback to the Celtic strain of Christianity. It was shortly after William the Conquerer invaded England in 1066, that builders started working on Durham Cathedral, and that is where St. Cuthbert's remains still lie today.

For centuries, pilgrims flocked to visit Durham and see Cuthbert's coffin, because of the reputation Bishop Cuthbert had made for himself as a healer, all those years ago. Archaeologists regard him as leaving a puzzling legacy, warrior or bishop, on the one hand, and then leaving pagan type jewellery which had been formed into a striking and unique Christian cross.

Hartlepool has always had close links with Durham, and in modern times it is part of the diocese of Durham. The much loved St.

Cuthbert probably met with St Hilda in her later years, and is always included along with the other saints that have influenced the town. As the crow flies, Durham Cathedral is only twenty miles away from Hartlepool Headland. For centuries the Bishops of Durham made great use of the Headland port because it was the biggest port in County Durham.

It was beside the port and on the site of St Hilda's monastery, that the Norman, Robert de Brus built St Hilda's church just a century after Durham Cathedral was built.

Chapter 3
THE VENERABLE BEDE

A portrait of Bede hangs with St Aidan and St Hilda and St Cuthbert, in the aisle of St Hilda's church, and he also features in a stained glass window on the North side of the church. Though separated from us by fifteen centuries or so, Jarrow is 30 miles to the north, and what Bede wrote there in his Ecclesiastical History about St Hilda in her first post as Abbess in Hereteu, now called Hartlepool, is amply en-forced by the archaeological digs on the Headland site. Then he tells how she was given land to build a second monastery in Streonshalch, or Whitby. These are the AngloSaxon place names that Bede used, and it is assumed confidently by histori-ans and scholars that they refer to Hartlepool and Whitby.

Elisabeth Westhead

He is a gift to historians because he writes so vividly. Thankfully he did not waste his time writing detective novels. Instead he painted lively pictures of the people all around him. When he says that St Hilda had an 'angelic face', we know that although he was too young to remember her himself, his colleagues will have known her when she was at Wearmouth monastery. So we are incredibly privileged to have such a very close link to the saints and the monks who lived and died virtu-ally under our feet at St Hilda's church.

Bede read and followed very early Christian historians, such as Eusebius, and he hoped that he was continuing to write with the same inspiration as they had. The seventh century, when the historian was alive and writing, was a time of great confusion and turbulence in England. He believed Christianity to be unifying force for good, which brought together the local tribes, and the recent Pagan settlers from Europe, namely Picts, Irish, Angles, Saxons, Jutes and Britons; so the overall theme of his writing was about moving from social diversity to unity, about uniting all the different warring factions that existed in Northern England in the seventh century.

Bede - the Venerable Bede as he is titled - was born in AD 673, just before Hil-da died in AD 680. He went to Wearmouth (Sunderland) monastery at the age of seven, where, it must be assumed, he learned to read and write and to work in Latin. (All his writings are in Latin, because, inconveniently, that was the best way to write things down. Runes were sometimes used, but use of the Roman alphabet to write early English was associated with King Aethelbert of Kent and only more widely adopted in the eighth century.) Having started monastic life as a little boy, he spent most of the rest of his life in a new monastic foundation in Jarrow, under the care of Abbot Ceolfrith, where he spent his time penning histories. 'The Ecclesi-astical History of the English People' is his best known work, but he wrote biogra-phies of Cuthbert and Wilfred, as well as 'Lives of the Abbots of Wearmouth and Jarrow'. Today he is regarded as England's first historian, since he not only related the facts, but shaped them, as historians do. He used this quote from Tacitus to show his purpose in writing: 'If history records good things of good men, the thoughtful reader's encouraged to imitate what is good; if it records evil of wicked men, the devout reader's encouraged to avoid all that is sinful and perverse'.

In those days, writing a book took months of craftsmanship, preparing the vellum - the animal skin - ready for writing, and making the inks in their different colours, and sharpening quills to make into pens. The books created by the Venerable Bede were not intended to be printed many times, of course, since printing had not been invented.

Elisabeth Westhead

There would be just one precious copy, deposited in a church or a monastery, and it would be only the monks and the priests who could actually read it. What made it harder still was the fact that books were all in Latin and not the language the people spoke. This meant that only an elite few could understand them and they had to be interpreted for the general public. The paper-back copies we have of his works today are helpfully translated into English and easy to obtain from Amazon or the town library. Without that support it would have taken so much longer to produce this little book!

Chapter 4
ABBESS HILDA

Hilda, our heroine, was born on 25th August AD 614, and spent the first 33 years of her life, living as a noblewoman, part of the Deiran royal family, and the latter 33 years living under religious orders. Modern historians call her Hild, (meaning battle). I shall call her Hilda throughout this little book because I am writing about a church called St. Hilda's which was named after her. I remember when Boadicea was re-named Boudicca. There seems to be a fashion in changing names for academic purposes.

At the age of 13, Hilda had been baptised by Paulinus into the Roman style of Christianity when he travelled North to York in Deira in AD 627 to baptise King Edwin and his household which included Hilda.(Paulinus built a wooden church in York and started the tradition which gave York a minster/cathedral and an archbishop, in later years.)

Over the border, in Bernicia, the Irish missionaries, Aidan and his monks, were arriving, and spreading a different brand of Christianity.

King Edwin was killed in battle, and the teachings of Paulinus disappeared with him. Oswald, King and latterly Saint, who succeeded Edwin, had been inspired in Scotland by the Celtic branch of Christianity. He united Deira and Bernicia and became the bretwalda - the overlord of both Deira and Bernicia. He knew about St Columba and the Irish Christians on Iona, so he chose to summon Irish Aidan, from Iona, hoping to persuade the people of Northumbria to adopt a Celtic form of Christianity.

Hilda was related to the royal families in both Northumbria, and East Anglia. She had been baptised in York, by Paulinus, brought up in Bamburgh in a pagan court, and then been influenced by Aidan at Lindisfarne. Her upbringing made her a good choice for the job of Abbess of Hartlepool. Introducing Christianity was regarded as partly a political move. And the way that the Celtic missionaries used to convert people, was that the faith would first be adopted by royalty and then would trickle down and spread out to the rest of the population.

At the age of 34, of her own accord, Hilda abandoned secular life and decided to serve God. Her original plans were to stay with her

Heart of the Headland

nephew, Aldwulf, King of East Anglia, and from there to go to France and join her sister, Hereswith, who was already settled as a nun and living in a monastery in Chelles, just south of Paris. However Hilda's plans were not going to work out.

Events took a sudden turn, when Bishop Aidan (recruited from Iona) requested her to return to the North, and gave her one hide of land on the North bank of the river Wear, (!Sunderland, Monkwearmouth?) where she lived as a nun with some companions for a year and started training for her new job. (In AD 645, there was no physical money, so payment was made in land, and one hide of land was an area big enough to graze one cow.) While women were often totally subservient to their husbands in the early Middle Ages, becoming Abbess of a monastery gave her land and power and a relatively comfortable life. For a seventh century woman, Hilda achieved remarkable power and respect. Her reputation for wisdom and people management shines on through the ages.

A nun called Heiu, (believed to be the Irish St Bega) had been made the first Abbess of the new monastery on Hartlepool Headland. She only stayed there briefly and then left to go to Kaelcacaestir (probably Tadcaster). This created a vacancy which Aidan urgently needed to fill.

So it was that, after only a year of monastic life, around AD 647, that Hilda was sent to replace Heiu, and thus in her thirties, she suddenly was made Abbess of Hartlepool. Bishop Aidan of Lindisfarne had great respect for Hilda, he admired her *'for her innate wisdom and love of God's service'*, as Bede put it. He therefore chose her as second Abbess of this new monastery, on Hartlepool Headland. King Oswy also had great confidence in Hilda and sent his daughter, Aelfflaed, to join the community in Hartlepool under the care of its abbess. Oswy had decided that the Christian God was the most powerful, and decided to dedicate his daughter to living a Christian life in a monastery.

Hilda continued to learn skills for the job with guidance from Bishop Aidan and others from Lindisfarne. The Island of Lindisfarne is about one hundred miles north of Hartlepool, and the journey by boat would not have been too difficult. Aidan could fairly easily have made visits offering support. Until AD 657 , that is, for nearly ten years, Hilda stayed in her post on Hartlepool Headland. Then the king offered her ten hides of land in Whitby.

Bede says very little about Hilda's character. She was obviously level-headed, and good at making decisions. We know she was loved by the monks because later in life they called her 'Mother'. Disappointingly, history tells us about the Synod, and about the ammonites in the cliffs, about the respect they all had for her, but no little personal querks.

Written history tells us no more about what happened to this monastery in Hartlepool, though it is thought that Hilda ran both monasteries simultaneously, continuing to oversee Hartlepool from Whitby Abbey. The trip by sea was much shorter for them, than for us who have to drive by road, cross the Tees flyover, and trek east over the moors. Archaeologists in the twentieth century, involved in excavating the Headland, think that (by examination of the artefacts found) the monastery survived on the Headland until the tenth century, but gradually declined as the Whitby monastic community eclipsed it. Because Royal and Continental influence was directed to the more southerly site of Whitby, it was that site that gained the prestige, and as the threat of Viking invasion became stronger this also made the Hartlepool community less attractive.

When Hilda moved to the larger site in Streonshalch (Whitby) - just as she had done in Hartlepool - 'she established a regular way of life and taught the observance of righteousness, mercy, purity, and other virtues, but especially of peace and charity'. Bede says that 'no-one in her monasteries was rich, no-one was needy, for everything was held in common and nothing was considered to be anyone's personal property'. Kings and princes used to come and ask her advice about their problems

Elisabeth Westhead

...and often they accepted what she said. Although little more is heard of Hartlepool, it was the habit of the Irish missionaries in spreading the Word, to build a network of communities. We must assume that these monasteries were networked together. Likewise, a daughter monastery at Hackness, near Scarborough had been established by the time of Hilda's death, and was probably similarly linked in.

When Whitby Abbey was first established, in AD 658, the monastery buildings were sited close to the port, but three miles from the North Sea. Over the centuries, the cliff has crumbled away and now the Abbey ruins look as though they are perched on a headland. The cliffs there on the Whitby coast are full of ammonite fossils. Hilda was reputed to have cast out snakes over the cliff tops, and the proof of this is evidenced by the ammonite fossils that still fall on the beach below. (Pope Gregory referred to the snake as a symbol of pagan worship, so this was a story with a very strong symbolism. The same story was told of St Patrick throwing snakes out of Ireland.)

While Hilda was Abbess in Whitby she oversaw the Synod, which would reshape Christianity in England for good. After King Oswald had been killed by Penda in battle, he was succeeded by Oswy. Now Oswy married a Catholic wife, and this was causing major disruption in the organisation of his court. It was not right that the Queen should be celebrating Easter while the King, in the same court, was still fasting for Lent. So for political as well as religious reasons, he asked Hilda if she would bring together representatives of both Roman and Celtic Christians to discuss the date of Easter, the hitch which seemed to be causing such major disruption. Since Easter was considered the most important festival in the Christian calendar, it was not fitting that the Celts and the Romans could not agree about setting the date. So it was that King Oswy approached Hilda to chair the Synod of Whitby in AD 664 because he admired her tact and good judgement.

I have given the Synod a chapter on its own. (See Chapter 5).

While Hilda was Abbess in Whitby, there was a man called Caedmon, who, when the harp was passed round for people to sing and entertain, would run away and hide in the cowshed because he felt inadequate. Then one day inspiration came to him and he created 'The Song of Creation', a poem in his native tongue. When he showed it to Hilda and the other monks they were all amazed at his new skill. After that, monks and priests came to him and read out tracts from the scripture, and he promptly translated them into poems in the vernacular, in his own tongue. This has been hailed as the beginning of Anglo-Saxon literature.

Elisabeth Westhead

It says a lot for Hilda's monastery in Whitby that five men from that institution in Whitby all ended up becoming bishops, including Wilfred, probably the best known of them.

After many years serving as Abbess, Hilda was struck by a burning fever, that racked her body continuously for six years. We know she did not make a fuss about her illness, since Bede recounts that *'during all this time she never ceased to give thanks to her Maker, or to instruct the flock committed to her, both privately and publicly'*. But after seven years, she finally succumbed. Our historian recounts that a nun, in a daughter institution in Hackness (near Scarborough), had a vision of Hilda's death, as it happened, and saw how *'her soul was borne up to heaven in the midst of light and accompanied and guided by angels.'* C.680 AD.

Hilda was succeeded by Aefflaed, daughter of the late King Oswald, as Abbess. We are told nothing about where St Hilda was finally laid to rest.

Chapter 5
THE SYNOD OF WHITBY. AD 664

Easter was considered the most important date in the Christian calendar, and both Kings and clergy - not to mention Bede - were unhappy that the Celtic church and the Roman church were not able to agree on its true place in the calendar. In the royal courts of the time, when the king and queen were of different traditions, then the court would feel forced to mark Easter twice, and one side would be still fasting for Lent while the other was celebrating Easter.

There were many differences between the Irish and Roman cultures. As an example, the Irish lived in villages with wooden thatched cottages and no built roads, while the Romans had stone buildings and used horses for travel. The Celts preferred simplicity, while the Romans regarded them as barbarians. It took St Augustine two years to travel from Rome to Kent, in the early seventh century, and once arrived, he was regarded with great suspicion by the King of Kent. The two met firstly in the open air instead of in a palace, because King Aethelberht of Kent suspected that Augustine might play magic tricks on him. So we find three belief systems, Paganism, Celtic Christianity and Roman Christianity all entangled in the minds of early seventh century royalty.

Some 60 years after Augustine arrived, King Oswy chose Hilda and her monastery in Whitby, as a place where the two Christian cultures could start to integrate. Even the common people were beginning to doubt Christianity when it showed splits like this. Oswy was keen to follow the Irish way although his queen was sure that the Roman teaching was true. Already there was considerable difference between the two trends, although is likely that the division at that time between Celts and Romans was not nearly as great as it became centuries later with the Renaissance, and with Henry VIII.

ABBOT Alchfrid, who had recently been given a monastery in Ripon (In-Hrypum) came with a priest named Agatho to represent the Roman point of view. King Oswy travelled from Northumberland, with Bishop Colman, to support Abbess Hilda and the Celtic side. Bishop Cedd came as interpreter, we are told....... Perhaps Colman having arrived on the scene only three years ago, spoke mainly Irish. We know also that the peasants spoke Anglo Saxon, and records were written in Latin, and we don't know how well the Roman Christians had converted from Italian to the vernacular. Perhaps they spoke mainly Latin........ Wilfred, living in Whitby Abbey, was asked and agreed to represent the Roman side because, Bede says, he spoke the local language better than Alchfrid.

The conference went on for days. Neither side wanted to make concessions, but it was a matter that had to be settled - and as amicably as possible. Bede tells how each side represented their views very tactfully. Both sides recalled the way they had been taught and the integrity of their teachers. Wilfred listened to the arguments of Colman. "Nor do I think that their ways of keeping Easter were seriously harmful, so long as no-one showed them a more perfect way to follow," said Wilfred. Still rather condescending, the Romans played on the remoteness of Ireland and the island of Iona, and questioned how people living so remotely could really know the truth better than Rome.

Finally the Irish had to agree that Jesus had given Pope Peter in Rome the keys of the Kingdom of heaven, and that Columba in Iona had not been given similar authority, and for this reason the Celtic believers felt they had to submit to the arguments of the Romans. This was a major decision in the history of Christianity. It arose in the first place, because the phases of the moon vary in different places on our planet. Oswy and Hilda managed successfully to make this momentous decision stick. They had agreed upon fixing the date of

Easter, satisfactorily. This was something that could be acted upon. Other customs and beliefs lingered on for many years because cultural practices are harder to change.

Now that he had lost the argument, Irish Bishop Colman took with him 30 or so monks, who all rejected the new Easter calculations, the different tonsure shapes, and other cultural considerations that had been discussed, and they returned together to Iona. Cedd, who had been converted to the Roman way, returned to his bishopric. It had been 30 years now since the Irish first came to Lindisfarne. They had set up a regime on the island where they owned little else but their cattle. Most of the money they received (according to Bede) they gave to the poor. And they continued their frugal practices in Northumbria for many years - in accordance with Celtic culture and as they had always done before.

We have to assume that Hilda was there presiding over this confrontation, not offering her views, but by her presence, keeping the confrontation civil. She belonged to the royal family and could therefore see why it was important for the two sides to come together and make this agreement. Yet the monastic environment which she had created in Hartlepool did not change too much despite the enormity of the final decision. In Whitby, there were more visits from Royalty. It was closer to continental ports, so archaeologists working in Whitby, found coinage, and evidence of European influence overcoming the Celtic origins.

The trouble that they experienced with the date of Easter was that it was dependent on the Moon. And the solar calendar is slightly longer than the 365 days of each year. In AD 664, Bede and scholars began to come to grips with this by creating leap years. The problem still was not solved. By the time of Henry VIII, the calendar was still four days out. Finally extra leap years were added at the turn of the centuries and thus the Gregorian calendar emerged in Italy in 1582, and was adapted in England in 1583. This is the calendar we still use today.

Chapter 6
ARCHAEOLOGY

It is hard for modern readers to imagine the importance of Northumbria in the seventh century, as ranked against the other seventh century kingdoms of this island. King Oswald had managed to unite Benicia and Deira, from The Firth of Forth to a boundary as far south as the Humber - that is from Edinburgh south to Hull. And this huge region was one of the most important kingdoms in Britain, and at the forefront of Christian decision making. So when Oswald appoints Irish Aidan to convert the warring tribes to Christianity, it is a big enough gesture to make the Pope in Rome feel threatened. Although the Synod of Whitby was to take place in Whitby, later on, what happened on this site was Irish-style, including the layout of the monastery and the construction of the buildings. Hilda's site in Whitby was different because it was much larger and came under a fair amount of pressure from the Continent.

Hartlepool excavations have not found gold or much jewellery. Their most significant finds were the eight 'namestones', - uniquely found in seventh century Bernicia. We have one in our church, so I will explain in full in the next chapter.

This is why the archaeological excavations on the headland are so important - because it is one of few sites which helps us to understand how Christianity was brought to this country from Ireland, and how it was set upon a course to trickle the faith down from royalty to the people through the establishment of monasteries.. St Bega (Heiu) and then St Hilda were the first women in the country to be given authority to run a monastery and be responsible for spreading Christianity. St Bega was elderly when she came, and soon left. St Hilda used her authority wisely. After learning her skills in Hartlepool, she moved to run Whitby Abbey as well. When she oversaw the Synod of Whitby, she made a permanent impression on the course of Christianity which lasts right through history until today.

The first of at least 36 archaeological excavations on the Headland was done in 1833 in the area of St Helen's Church near the narrowest part of land alongside the modern exit road. Not much is known about St Helen's. But later excavation work was to uncover more about St Hilda's monastery, which was the most important area in the middle of the Headland. In 1833, house builders found two namestones from the cemetery at Cross Close (near the seaward end of Baptist Street). Some of the female skeletons there were found with their heads resting on small stone squares. Other stones were engraved and some plain. The best preserved of the engraved namestones is on permanent display in the church today.

It was excavating the cemeteries that gave archaeologists the best clues as to how life was organised on the Headland. The Saxon buildings were of wood and thatch and mainly rotted away with time. But the women's cemetery had these namestones, and some of the graves in the men's cemetery were edged by a semicircle of stones.

Today, St Hilda's Church, built of local stone still stands on the site at the height of the ridge where we think our earliest predecessors placed their wooden church. When installing underfloor heating recently, in the church, historians were delighted to find a post hole, which aligned with another post hole outside the church to the north, indicating a large Saxon building which could have been St Hilda's church.

The bones of a seventh-century nun are buried under a marked slab in the chancel of the modern St Hilda's Church. She was found during recent BBC excavations and relocated. East/west rows of skeletons

Heart of the Headland

with their heads all facing north were found buried in Cross Close. This was the site where the seventh century female monks lived and had their cemetery. She was one of these. There are also Franciscan friars under the chancel, from a later monastic community which settled to the west of the church.

Elisabeth Westhead

The Durham University team of archaeologists worked out a plan of the Headland, which shows how the peninsular was laid out by St Bega and St Hilda. The men's dormitories and also their cemetery was in the area of Church Close, on the corner of the road opposite the North entrance to the church. The Anglo Saxon church, a wooden structure, most likely was positioned on the highest point of the ridge where St Hilda's Church stands today.. Then St Hilda, or the Abbess had a small room and sleeping quarters nearby, and the female monks lived further away in Cross Close on the seafront with their own cemetery. A big enclosed area owned by the monks, presumable for grazing animals or growing crops, stretched North, away down the limestone ridge to the Moor. And it was the custom of these Irish monasteries to encourage crafts such as house-building, thatching or beekeeping to teach the local population better skills. So there will have been a craft shed on the site as well. A beautifully worked metal lamb was found in Hartlepool.

It was hard for the archaeology team to be sure what they were discovering, since the buildings were all of wood with thatched roofs, so they left little trace for those digging fourteen centuries later. But the AngloSaxon monks used pots, which broke sometimes, and they discarded animal bones and dropped ornaments and crucially sank doorposts into the soil, which left imprints. They also had tools, which all gave clues to where they lived. It is possible nowadays even to know what they ate - lamb and pork, poultry, and wild birds, fishes and seafood, carrots, wild garlic, onions, leeks and legumes. They made bread and stews , flavoured with herbs and honey. Cider and mead and beer were drunk, though no wine, for wine-making skills had been lost when the Romans left.

Their buildings were rectangular, with a hearth for cooking food and providing light. The rich, and perhaps the invalids, slept on wooden beds, with a woollen stuffed mattress. Their clothes were of wool. The Prior of Durham kept large flocks of sheep at the mouth of the Tees, where Seal Sands and Able shipyards are to be found now. Perhaps some of the wool for clothes came from these sheep.

We have no evidence that Hartlepool and Whitby produced manuscripts such as the Venerable Bede in Jarrow did, since nothing has survived, though it seems likely that influenced by Bede and inspired by Lindisfarne, writing manuscripts and bookmaking and illumination skills would be crafts they encouraged.

Strangely, only a few years after Tees Archaeology came to Hartlepool, in the twenty-first century, the archaeologist, Steve Sherlock was excavating fields at Street Houses between Loftus and the sea, where he found evidence of many layers of ancient settlements. Between AD 2005 and AD 2010 he made his most exciting discovery - the bed burial of a Saxon Princess, which he dated to approximately AD 650. Bed burials are very rare and given only to the highest ranks in society, and this unnamed lady had golden jewellery and accoutrements that showed she was both royal and Christian. It seems likely that she was Royalty and that Hilda knew her. A pilgrimage route passes close to this site.

Aidan and his monks did not choose these remote sites in isolation. It was important that there were backup resources inland. West and South of the Headland there were the Roman settlements of Hart and Catcote, which have also been investigated by local archaeology teams, a few miles inland, which will have provided the Hartlepool monastery, with help in case of attack, food in case of harvest failure and so on.

Chapter 7
THE PORT

Hartlepool.

In medieval times people used the sea much more frequently than we do as a means of transport. Aidan will have travelled to Hartlepool to see Hilda - by boat. Similarly Hilda will have travelled to Whitby and her monks with her... by boat. The Newport Bridge and the Transporter bridge were nineteenth century triumphs, and before that the River Tees will have constituted a major obstacle to travellers. There was perhaps a ferry across the Tees for many years, used by those monks, who travelled on foot along the coast from Whitby to Hartlepool and vice versa, but, as long as one could navigate the ancient sunken forests hidden in Hartlepool coastal waters, sea was the obvious way to travel. It is not known for certain that the Celts and the Anglo Saxons had sailing skills. However, it is thought that since much older civilisations than the monks at Linsisfarne were able to sail across the Mediterranean, and the Vikings were seasoned sailors, we assume that Aidan and Hilda also could sail. On the whole, throughout the ages, the Headland would have been an insignificant backwater were it not for its port.

When William the Conqueror took power in 1066, one of the first things he did was to survey the defences of the island. He very soon realised that the Picts were a major problem to the North of England and that he could not deal with this from his base in the South. So it was very early in his reign, that he granted to the Bishop of Durham the right to summon an army. Durham remains a Palatinate with Prince Bishops keeping their rights as princes even in the twenty-first century.

Heart of the Headland

Hartlepool was a centre for much fighting on the North East coast……. (Isle of Hild p 13) over the centuries, because of its large port. And of course, the port was a good source of revenue for the Headland. When the port was abandoned and left to silt up, then the fortunes of the church and the little town, declined as well.

As long as it remained the only port in Durham, it was treasured by the Prince Bishops. In 1173, it is recorded, the nephew of the Bishop of Durham landed at Hartlepool with 40 knights and 500 foot soldiers in order to fight the raiding Scots. (P 23 History of Hartlepool, Sir Cuthbert Sharp). Luckily, the Scottish King, William, had been taken prisoner in Alnwick much further north, on this occasion, so it turned out there was no need for the little army the Bishop had assembled. All the same, it is impressive that Hartlepool, at that time, had a port big enough to disembark so many troops.

The power of the Durham Palatinate, and the fear of Scottish raids, account for the fact that for centuries the Headland was protected by a sea wall long enough to need three gates. Nowadays only one gate remains in the medieval sea wall, and the port has moved west and been dredged out for much larger shipping. For years, though, the landing stage will have been the quayside just close to the church and the fear of the Vikings and then the Scots will have been very real.

Elisabeth Westhead

Situated as it was, the port was just a stone's throw from the church, and Hartlepool Headland was important to the Prince Bishop of Durham for centuries. Then with improved technology, the River Tees was cleared of obstructions and the Bishop of Durham found himself a new port on the Tees in 1680. The consequences of this for Hartlepool were bad. The fortunes of the Headland declined, and in 1720, as you will read below, the parishioners had to raise serious money to repair the church. St Hilda's continues to the present day to remain in the diocese (administrative area) of Durham. In 1808, (Cuthbert Sharp P151), the harbour was sold to a man who enclosed it and used it for agriculture, it had become so silted up.

Roughly speaking, the population of the headland grew slowly as seamen and fishermen came to live there. There were times when the port prospered and then the church was well looked after, then there were lean times when the people had hardly enough to look after themselves, and the church was allowed to fall into decay.

In AD 1714, Hartlepudleans requested that the judges at the quarter sessions would recommend to Her Majesty, Queen Anne, to grant letters patent for the repair of the church. They had to put out another reminder, and it was 1719 before anything happened, and finally it was King George who gave Hartlepool a brief to collect '£1732 and upwards' to repair and rebuild the church.

By 1719, the church was in a lamentable state. 'The choir being at present almost entirely unroofed and the steeple's (Tower's?) pillars and walls of the same so much decayed by length of time that the whole fabric will inevitably fall to the ground unless speedily prevented by taking down and re-building some and repairing the decayed parts thereof.' (Cuthbert Sharp. P114). Finally money was found and repairs were started in 1721. On this occasion, there was not enough money raised to repair the whole church and most of the work was done on the Nave, leaving the East and West ends to crumble.

Again in 1924, after the whole of Hartlepool had experienced a boom and the town had briefly been the chief port in the country, at the end of the nineteenth century, funding was found to reconstruct the extremities of St Hilda's. The chancel and the Galilee chapel were beautifully re-designed and rebuilt by W.H.Caroe, a big firm of London architects, and so today we have a large spacious church, which has withstood the wild weather of the North Sea, but needs constant funding to keep it still standing safely.

The port now, in the twenty-first century, has been properly dredged, and is deep enough to harbour quite large freight, and also hosts a

Elisabeth Westhead

business that builds and services North Sea oil rigs. It is administered in conjunction with Teesside port, and is sometimes described as the 'jewel in the crown' of the local shipping industry.

Chapter 8
THE FRIARY

After the monastery of St Bega and St Hilda had faded away, there was another religious group that set up on the Hartlepool Headland. They were members of the Franciscan order, founded by St Francis, a mendicant order, wearing grey hooded gowns. These greyfriars arrived in the middle of the thirteenth century, as the church was being constructed nearby. And this new monastic group was probably set up by Robert de Brus VI, still with an eye on keeping the land in de Brus ownership.

The Friary of Hartlepool near the Town Moor, was only dissolved in the 37th year of the reign of Henry VIII, at the time of Henry's Dissolution of the Monasteries, and it is recorded that at that time there was one keeper with eighteen brothers. A portrait of the last master of the friary, a drawn and lined face, hangs in the church, Richard Threlkeld. A new building called the Friarage was built after the suppression of the monasteries in AD 1605. Some bones of the friars that were found in archaeological excavation, have been placed under the chancel of St Hilda's, near the remains of the nun from the Cross Close cemetery of Hilda's monastery.

Part of this old Friarage Manor House AD 1605, still stands on Friarage Field. It is Grade II listed. It was once preserved as part of the interior of the hospital. But the hospital has now been pulled down and the Manor House still remains.

Chapter 9
ARCHITECTURE

The Church is built like a beacon on the highest point of the limestone ridge of the Headland, on the foundations of a twelfth century church, and also on the site where archaeologists believe St Bega had positioned her monastery church in AD 647. Where it stands, it is visible from the sea and all around, and represents a symbol of the Christian faith dating back into history and carrying forward the responsibility for all its history, hopefully into a new future of hope and creativity.

St Hilda's is not an elegant structure with a tall spire soaring heavenwards. It is more of a motherly building with an unstable and clumsily buttressed tower, and rows of symmetrical clerestory windows. The tower has always been unstable, and it is now not completely vertical. A bulge can be seen, at its north-west corner. Throughout the last 800 years, much effort has been expended in trying to prop it up. Nikolaus Pevsner, architect and writer, after carefully examining the unstable tower, suggested that the original tower might have been designed to be at the centre of a cruciform structure when it was first built, which would have stabilised it. For some reason, the intended two arms extending north and south were not built, which meant the massive buttresses had to be erected instead to stabilise the tower.

The long building stretches modestly through the churchyard featuring several different entrances. Unusually the church has a Galilee chapel, built for the Lord of the Manor to hold court cases, but now houses the gas boiler and the toilets! The entrance is worn, but the ceiling is very grand! Today's visitors walk through a very old archway, through the Galilee chapel and into the hospitality area at the back of the church. A glass inner door is planned to improve disabled access, and also a glass meeting room to be built in 2025.

As you walk inside that you realise how light and spacious it is, with Early English pillars lacing the nave and the amazing arch stretching up above the high altar. The stained glass windows enhance the general effect letting plenty of light stream through onto the 12th century floor, with the line of clerestory windows providing extra illumination from high above.

After 1066, the Norman invaders constructed churches and cathedrals both for their personal salvation, and in order to take

Heart of the Headland

spiritual domination over the nation. St Hilda's was built about a century after Durham Cathedral. The Bishop of Durham had been made a Prince Bishop, and given powers to raise an army to use against the Pictish raids, and the Prince Bishops were keen to use Hartlepool Headland as their port when needed. Durham Cathedral and the castle stood just 20 miles inland, and the bishops' use of the port brought wealth to the area.

Robert de Brus was a nobleman who came from Normandy with William the Conqueror. The new king gave him land in Skelton, North Yorkshire, and the Manor of Hart which included the Hartlepool Headland. He built the Priory and the parish church in Guisborough, then his son Robert de Brus II built St Hilda's on the Headland. Like many noblemen of his time, they probably built these churches to stop their land being split by inheritance. And the sarcophagus in the de Brus chapel of St Hilda's, below the East window, is thought to be the resting place of some members of the de Brus family.

The nave of St Hilda's church has remained much as it was built in the thirteenth century, while the tower, the Galilee chapel and the chancel (that is both ends of it !) have been repaired and reconstructed over the years.

Heart of the Headland

St Hilda's is built in the pale cream Magnesian limestone, which was quarried out to deepen the port area. Here and there, recent repairs to the church building can be seen where yellow limestone from the surrounding area has been used. One obvious example is a yellow stone that can be found low on the outside of the South wall of the Galilee chapel, the wall facing the car park.

St Hilda's monastery may only have finally declined in the tenth century, the archaeologists suggest, so the gap in time was not huge between the decline of the old monastery and the building of the modern St Hilda's church. Then out to the west of the Anglo-Saxon site, when the monastery had faded away, the de Brus family founded a friary with Franciscan friars. It was, after all, common practice for the nobility to provide grants in the form of land for religious foundations.

Although Durham Cathedral is only a century older than St Hilda's, the architectural differences are stark. The pillars in the main part of the Cathedral are massive cylindrical Norman pillars with geometrical patterns on them. The pillars in St Hilda's are in what is called Early English style (sometimes described as Gothic). Much more elegant. They form six bays in the nave, rising to pointed arches. The interior of the roof in Hartlepool is wooden, so relatively light and not requiring the same support as the Durham Cathedral roof.

The columns in the nave and the windows are probably the most striking features of the church. The earlier north side pillars are a little shorter than their opposites on the south side, where the arches are decorated with little triangles, in what is called a nutmeg pattern. The archway in the chancel, opposite the organ, which frames the window depicting St Hilda, has an enhanced nutmeg pattern. There is interesting decoration at the top of some pillars, too. Where the nave meets the choir, the pillars are topped with waterleaf carvings. Waterleaf carvings depict vertical leaves, curling outwards at the top of the capitals. It was a pattern used in France, thought to be brought across the Channel by Cistercian monks around 1180. Because this pattern is used in Fountains Abbey as well as St Hilda's, it is thought we probably shared the same Master Builder. And where two arches form a triangle with the roof, in the chancel, there are

little patterns which John Barnes, our architect, describes as 'clock faces in spandrels'.

The high windows above the nave are tall, narrow and pointed at the top, clerestory windows in lancet shape. They run along the topmost wall sections of the nave, lighting up the space below quite magically. Outside the church, the lancet windows are built into a pattern that cannot be seen from the interior, arranged in threes, all around the church, each glass window flanked either side by a blind window. This creates a nice structural rhythm all around the church. To enrich the effect, they are flanked by an 'en lit' design - that is extra little vertical pillars either side. Cuthbert Sharp, the Hartlepool historian and architect, really hated lancet windows, and complains about them at length in his History of Hartlepool - on aesthetic grounds!

The stained glass is mainly nineteenth century, 1860 and onwards, generously donated by wealthier members of the congregation and incomers. A lovely picture of our patron, St Hilda, as a young woman, decorates the south side of the chancel. There is an appealing picture of the Young Christ to her left, with the face of a young member of the Boys Brigade and the Headland foreshore behind. Then, also of special significance, there is a portrait of St Bega, Irish princess of the seventh century, in a brown cloak with a green sash. Along the northern wall, also featured in glass are the rest of our favoured saints - a second portrait of St Hilda, The Venerable Bede, St Aidan, and St Cuthbert.

Mid nineteenth century was an exciting time for colour. Where once onions were used for yellow dye and spinach for green, suddenly there was a breakthrough in the chemistry of colour. It affected embroidery silk, wallpaper, fabrics....... Heaton of Heaton, Butler and Bayne, in the capital, had discovered over one hundred and thirty colours they could use for making stained glass, (See Appendix.) and the Rev Ormsby, the incumbent at the time, was inspired to bring their discoveries here to the north to illustrate the wonderful reds, yellows, oranges and browns that were possible, all glowing brightly in St Hilda's stained glass. Stained glass had never been so exciting since medieval times!

On various occasions, over the years, the building has fallen into serious disrepair and the people of Hartlepool have had to find funding somehow in order to restore it, as in 1719, when they petitioned George I. Then other major repairs were done in the nineteenth and twentieth centuries adding the organ and one by one the stained glass windows. (See appendix.) The German bombardment, in December 1918, caused so much damage elsewhere on the Headland, but just once hit St Hilda's and thankfully did only minor shrapnel damage to the roof on the north side. It wasn't until 1924 after a substantial donation from William Grey, shipbuilders, that W. H. Caroe, architects, finally repaired the Galilee chapel and the choir and chancel.

The current East window is only partially filled with stained glass reflecting the sad history of the church. There had been a wall erected, truncating the chancel, with a smallish East window, which stood during the eighteenth and nineteenth centuries when subscriptions had been inadequate to rebuild the de Brus chapel. Then when Caroe redesigned the East end with its wonderful arches, the new window was much larger than the old substitute East window had been, and the stained glass was transferred from the small old window to the large new one, and the extra space was filled with plain glass. It covers the Life of Christ quite comprehensively but rather haphazardly.

It is the detail put in by the Twelfth century stone masons, and the addition of such brilliant windows, and a large electrically operated organ, (see appendix for details) which leave us, some eight hundred years later, a valuable, beautiful, and much loved- but quite fragile- monument, which is ours to support and enjoy, but is still a heavy responsibility to maintain.

Elisabeth Westhead

Chapter 10

NAME-DROPPING A TOUR INSIDE THE CHURCH

This chapter is about people who donated to the church and people whose names crop up as one walks round St Hilda's. I have chosen this Chapter, too, to explore theories about the Namestone displayed in the St Nicholas' Chapel.

It is a dog-friendly church. People occasionally bring well-behaved pooches which sit through the services. People also arrive on bicycles and can leave them in the Galilee chapel. Great efforts are made to include everyone.

The main entrance through the porch hides a beautiful and very ancient Norman archway with chevron moulding. Sadly it is only occasionally used because the levels of the church floor and the ground outside are different, and the steps which were built to help the able-bodied churchgoers to reach ground level are impossible for wheelchair users to navigate. Further help for wheelchair users to enter, is planned in the near future, when the heavy oak doors at the west end will be pinned back.

All the incumbents, from when the church was first built, are listed on the board at the back. They number about fifty-five, starting with two Norman priests, Joh. de Wyrksall and Joh. de Couton (1353). One unusual feature on this list of rectors and curates is that the second female priest listed, Patricia Webster was mother of Verity Joy Brown, the third female priest.

The font was donated in 1728 by George Bowes (sometime mayor) and his wife, whose daughter, Mary Eleanor married John Lyon, Earl of Strathmore, from which came The Queen Mother's surname: Bowes-Lyon.

There are windows in the chancel depicting a boat in the distance behind the Young Christ, and another of Christ arriving in a boat. If the money in the church had come from the local people, from fishermen and seafarers, then sea-faring ships might have been better represented in the windows. Most of the benefactors, like the mayors, came into Hartlepool from outside, and our beautiful stained glass was often installed in memory of their loved ones. (See appendix.)

Jane Bell has a brass plaque on the north wall. She was married to

Heart of the Headland

Perceval Bell (Mayor) and died in 1594. She is commemorated for her generous donations to the church.

It was Conacher of Hull in 1871, who built a mechanical organ for the church, then it was rebuilt in 1930 with pneumatic action, and finally was restored with electric action in 1990. See Appendix for more details.

The grand piano belonged to BBC Glasgow until they went digital. Fortuitously, Ian Pounder, the organist, traced it to auction in Leeds and bought it for us. It is used for concerts, and if there is a problem with the organ, or the choir are singing some gentler music.

Because the de Brus tomb was left exposed to the elements for centuries, the inscription on it became almost illegible, so when the Rev. Todd looked at the worn inscription on the tomb in the de Brus chapel he suggested that it read : "Bulmer", and not : "de Brus". But since the sarcophagus lies in the de Brus chapel, in a church built by Robert de Brus II, it seems safe to assume that the sarcophagus actually belongs to the de Brus family.

There is a photo on display of Edward VIII visiting the church after the major reconstruction work of 1924 while he was Prince of Wales, before he became King.

Elisabeth Westhead

A small niche in the wall, three quarters of the way up the south side, which has a fragment of the bowl itself in it, is all that is left of the holy water stoup. Just to the left of the stoup , a former priests' entrance is bricked up.

Sir Cuthbert Sharp, a local eighteenth-century architect, built his house very close to the West end of the church, and a photo hanging on the North wall shows. His major contribution to the Headland and St. Hilda's was his book: 'History of Hartlepool', a much respected and comprehensive work which has been updated and re-printed several times.

One 'slave' is recorded as having been baptised in the church. Being as hardly anyone in Hartlepool was rich enough to have servants, it is possible that this 'slave' was servant to one of the Mayors or donors of the time. It will have been most strange to see a black face on Hartlepool Headland.

The church has a small choir, and its members are allowed to wear red gowns because of the church's royal connection.

From 1884, Dr A.E. Morrison was the guiding influence of the 1st Hartlepool Boys Brigade , the first brigade in an English town. The portrait of the young Christ in the chancel window was created to celebrate the beginning of the movement in Hartlepool. It was like the Boy Scouts, but founded earlier, and the brigade members had to attend church once a month. It proved to be a very popular organisation, and old photos of their parades show just how numerous they were. Members of the Boys Brigade and the Girls Brigade still attend church once a month. Ever since Whitsuntide 1891, the brigades have been making their annual camp in the grounds of Castle Howard. The Girls' Brigade was formed shortly after the Boys' Brigade!

Billy Purvis, Clown, the King o'Tyne and Grand Jester of the North (d.1853) is buried in the churchyard.

What happened to the wood when the pews were replaced by chairs? The wood was only of poor quality pine, so it was auctioned off to the congregation as firewood or for souvenirs.

In 2000 when the church was re-furbished, the rood screen was removed from the chancel and refitted behind the font. This exposed the waterleaf carving to advantage. And it gave the church architect the opportunity to introduce the modern Alpha and Omega hanging sculpture, which replaced the old green and gold cross, and subtly echoed the pattern of the namestone.

Elisabeth Westhead

THE NAMESTONE

In archaeological and historical terms - the most important stone in the church is the 'namestone'.

I make the argument below that this was St Hilda's stone, and that she was buried in Hartlepool. There is no proof. This is just a theory. What ever the truth, this stone has survived thirteen centuries underground remarkably well, and in itself is rare and valuable evidence from the days of Hartlepool's Celtic Christian monastery. If it didn't belong to St Hilda herself, then at the very least we can be sure it belonged to a royal relative or a colleague of hers. It is only a piece of stone - but arguably the Heart of the Headland.

In 1833, builders were in Cross Close, digging the foundations of a house for John Bulmer, when they found the first "Namestone". Altogether, one by one, in the course of several 'digs' nine Hartlepool namestones were excavated, eight in Cross Close, and a ninth one

Heart of the Headland

that seemed to fit the same Hartlepool pattern was brought from Billingham. The best preserved and most beautiful of the namestones is illuminated in an oak case near the chancel. The other eight were shared out to museums round the country.

Recent archaeology has confirmed that St Hilda's monastery had two cemeteries, one for men, near the North entrance to the church and one for women at Cross Close beside the sea. The 'nuns' were all buried with their heads to the North, feet to the South, which differs from modern Christian custom, but this was very early. In the seventh century, British Christianity was still developing the icons and the customs which are so familiar to us today. Some of them, in the Northern area of the cemetery, had their heads lying on plain small flat stones 4" or 5" square, like pillows. Archaeologists named these : "pillow stones".

With a few of the skulls were larger, carved, flat stones approximately 11.5 inches square. (Archaeologists cannot decide exactly how these carved stones were placed.) These nine inscribed stones were catalogued in 1984 by Professor Rosie Cramp of Durham University. Our stone is the best preserved and was numbered "1" of the collection. They were divided by a cross into four sections, you can see an Alpha and an Omega in the top two quadrants, representing God.

Elisabeth Westhead

Then excitingly, in the lower quadrants of each namestone, is carved a name, in runes. The stone on display in St Hilda's is of dolomite, (from the Sunderland quarry, perhaps) and the name carved on it is: HILDITHRYTH, which could mean Hilda the Strong. Another of the stones read: HILDIGYTH, possibly Hilda the Generous. It suggests that there were two Royal "Hilda"s buried in Hartlepool. I think it possible that the names were in two parts, firstly the given name, then the second half of the inscription, or the suffix, being added to describe the deceased. The Anglo-Saxon expert of 1886, Mr Bosworth, referred to the suffix as an encomium.

Stone was rarely used in seventh century Anglo-Saxon Bernicia. It was found neither on Celtic Christian sites, nor in buildings, so this was something very special, and still not properly understood. Runes were a Scandinavian or Germanic form of writing using straight lines to make it easier to carve on stone. We can see that this inscriber was not used to writing runes, and had problems spelling, since there is an X over GYTH, on the stone, to mark a mistake! It was probably an amateur filling in the name on a pre-prepared stone.

The fact that they made the effort to use stone, buried with some of the skeletons at the northern end of this little cemetery, showed that the deceased had been important people of high birth. Other similar stones with their own variant patterns, have been found in Billingham, some in Wearmouth, and some similar in Lindisfarne. Yet others recently have been found in Shannon, in Ireland. The stones were neither headstones or gravestones, and definitely not the overground markers we nowadays call gravestones. They were only eleven inches square, and found almost uniquely in Bernicia. So they are described as: "Namestones."

Not even Whitby Abbey in Deira has 'namestones'. It is possible that they characterised the Celtic Christianity that arrived with Aidan, which would explain why the only other place where namestones have only been recorded is in Ireland.

I am not the first to suggest that Hilda could have been buried in Hartlepool, and my argument goes like this:

Firstly, she was of royal birth, so she would have been given a namestone, had she been buried in Cross Close.

Secondly, it is likely she was Abbess over both monasteries simultaneously, even after she moved to the new abbey in Streonshalch/Whitby, so she would not have lost her connection to the smaller site of Hartlepool. Over the years, Whitby had become less Celtic and more European in lifestyle. Even the layout of the site was more Roman and less Celtic. Hilda seemed to prefer the Celtic ways.

Thirdly, Abbess Hilda died after a long illness, during which she would have had time to consider where she wanted her body to rest. As there is nothing to tell us where Hilda was buried, and we know that she tended to prefer the old Celtic ways to the new Roman Christianity, it is quite possible that she was brought back to Hartlepool to be buried in Cross Close, at her first monastery.

In which case, the dolomite stone HILDITHRYTH or "Hilda the Strong", could well have been the namestone denoting the resting place of St Hilda herself.

On the shores of the Black Sea, in Caucasian Georgia, the Georgian Orthodox Church pays homage to St Nino, who brought Christianity to the country making a symbolic cross out of leaning vine twigs - in the fourth century AD.

Christianity took longer to arrive in England in Bernicia, Three centuries after St Nino, We read about St Aidan and St Hilda bringing Christianity to Northern England. When Aidan chose Heiu and Hilda to set up the monastery on the Headland, it was just the dim beginnings of Christianity in England, and our church, St Hilda's, on the Headland,

Heart of the Headland

carries a message - from fourteen centuries ago - through this stone found on the Headland. The Alpha and the Omega symbolise the Christian God. The immature Runic writing on the stone comes from a civilisation that was only just learning to write their own language,. The stone is displayed in the church, only yards from where it was found, and it represents a Christian message to us, from a nun called Hilda, maybe St Hilda herself, who lived on the Headland 14 centuries ago, with a carving as crisp and new as if it had just been cut. A Christian message from a thatched wooden church to today's Grade 1 listed building......

Chapter 11
PILGRIMAGE ROUTES

The Way of Love and The Way of St Hild are modern pilgrimage routes. They roughly follow the ancient routes, and make the same connections - Headland to Whitby, travelled by St Hilda's monks, and Headland to Durham, travelled in reverse by the Durham bishops looking for a port to use.

Heart of the Headland

Some of the monks would travel from Whitby Abbey to Hartlepool Abbey and back, on foot. Perhaps there was a ferry over the River Tees where now the Transporter Bridge stands. I see this as a parallel to the Spanish monks of California who walked along the Pacific coast, stopping at monasteries, with names like San Diego, San Francisco, Santa Barbara, Santa Monica, not to mention San Jose. When the third monastery of the series was set up in Hackness near Scarborough, this will have been a new daughter monastery and the monks will have walked there as well. Although the monks will have walked, the Abbess, Royalty and perhaps the infirm, probably sailed.

In the early twenty-first century, archaeologist, Steven Sherlock uncovered a rare 'bed burial' near Loftus. The Saxon Princess buried there died in the seventh century, circa 650, with engraved gold jewellery, and artefacts that showed her to be Christian. Archaeologists have assumed that she was known to St Hilda. Since she had set up her household in that spot on the coast, and was an early Christian, it is a reasonable assumption that she was known to St Hilda or even related to her, despite the fact that archaeology cannot tell us precisely who she was; and her place would have made another stopping point on the journey from one Abbey to the other.

Elisabeth Westhead

It was in about 2023, the two pilgrimage routes were set up, starting from St Hilda's church. The Way of St Hild, routes pilgrims along the coast, passing RSPB Saltholme, near Streethouses, site of the the Saxon Princess find, and past Easington and Lythe churches both of which have a collection of Saxon stones. Since both Easington and Lythe churches stand at the top of major hills, it is likely that Easington and Lythe offered rest and refreshment to monks travelling from Whitby to Hartlepool.

Heart of the Headland

The Way of Love winds deep into the countryside, via Saxon Hart church and the old church in Trimdon Village to descend steeply into Durham, past a Nature Reserve, then walking along the river to finally reach Durham Cathedral. People like to walk along these pilgrimage routes...... taking a leisurely pace on foot through the countryside, instead of driving, so they can visit the churches and maybe dream of times gone by. They can expect to find stone echoes of the people who passed that way before. I see these paths as another link to our Anglo-Saxon past and part of the network of associations that all link in to St Hilda. We live lives of great leisure now, in contrast to the monks of St Hilda's monastery. These routes represent a different means of recalling St Hilda, St Cuthbert and all the Christians who trod those paths centuries ago.

Chapter 12

THE ROLE OF THE CHURCH IN THE TWENTY-FIRST CENTURY

The Venerable Bede spent his life writing about Christianity in the hope that it would be a community asset, and capable of bringing together the warring tribes arriving from the continent. St Hilda as Abbess gave herself a responsible social role in the community, as well as delivering her religious role, teaching skills and crafts, encouraging Caedmon to compose poetry in the vernacular instead of the usual Latin. This educational role was expected in Celtic monasteries. Simon Jenkins on a recent radio broadcast about cathedrals said how the attendance at cathedrals was growing, not just for Christian services, but also for offering space to the community they serve, allowing local universities to make use of the space, for example. For these buildings belong to our heritage and we need to find ways to maintain them. While on the same day, on the other side of the world, 87-year-old Pope Francis was on a visit to a remote jungle area of Papua New

Heart of the Headland

Guinea, where (according to The Independent) he aimed *'to promote civic responsibility, co-operation and an end to violence in the area'* as well as spreading love among the Faithful.

Civilisation has moved on since the time of Bede. We have inherited beautiful stone buildings to cherish, instead of seventh century wooden churches. Technology has advanced, but humans have not changed much since then.

In 2020-22 the pandemic unsettled many civilisations across the world. The threat of climate change is becoming increasingly challenging. The north east of England is no longer the important place it was in seventh century England, so I am picking out some of the social grievances that drive today's unrest in the area immediately surrounding the Headland.

Sometimes protesters do not even know what fuels their rage.

I am writing this soon after the summer riots in England, which started off in Hartlepool in 2024. It is thought that this episode of dissatisfaction was sparked off by a blogger writing false racist information on the internet! following a serious stabbing incident in Southport. The seven cities in England where the rioting took place are all in the list of the ten most deprived places in the country. These are places typically where people have no more hope, no trust in politicians, fear of what the future will bring, people who feel unable to keep themselves clothed, fed and alive and provide for themselves to the standard they would like or to the standards they see others keeping.

All over the country young couples are stuck living with their parents because they cannot afford their own property. In the poorest areas like West Hartlepool there are huge buildings like former cinemas and public service buildings, just falling into disrepair and crumbling bricks onto public roads sometimes. And then there are areas burnt out by casual arsonists, often teenagers. It is not infrequent that the mainline services that run through the countryside nearby, are delayed because of a person on the tracks. One immediately thinks: " Not another suicide? Just one more person who cannot cope?" Farmers are giving up because they cannot get fair prices for their products, because of supermarket bargaining power and foreign competition. Fishermen are in despair on this coast and round the Headland because starfish and shellfish are found mysteriously washed up dead on the beaches.

So perhaps is little wonder that people have so much anger. The summer riots of 2024 saw mothers urging their children to throw bricks at the police - for no simple reason. Burning wheelie bins were used as

Heart of the Headland

weapons. Teenagers set police cars on fire. My immediate reaction was: "This is England! We are a phlegmatic people. Why is this happening here?"

Then only a couple of miles from the centre of the rioting, we were awarded huge sums for the preservation of this ancient and beautiful building. Why should the church get such money? Should we be giving to the poor instead, and letting the building fall into ruins? This is bound to cause some jealousy.

There is no easy answer. Rather than add one more ruined building to the torched Wesleyan Chapel, and the smashed Art Deco building at the traffic lights, it makes sense to preserve beautiful ancient monuments like St Hilda's and work to maintain a legacy which dates back centuries. Our ancestors bothered to make the town a pleasant place for us, after all. It is only worthwhile to spend money on it, and then guarantee that the church is a positive asset to the community it serves. It is to be hoped that the church goers are aware of their privileged status, and will open up to the poorer and disadvantaged members of the community. How could it happen in this age of cynicism, without appearance of condescension?

Elisabeth Westhead

It seems right that accepting big sums of money to maintain our heritage should be balanced by a strong sense of community awareness - bringing everyone in from outside to enjoy our precious space, the peace, and the heritage that has been gifted to us through over 800 years of history. We should probably feel some sense of moral obligation. In order to justify receiving this funding for upkeep, the church needs to reach out to the community, in any way it can, to mend social wounds, cool the anger, demonstrate caring and compassion......

A task that is easier said than done. However it must be our sacred duty to try! It is only in this spirit that we can move forward with a clear conscience, observing our duty to our forbears as well as to future generations, and continuing the legacy of St Hilda and the Venerable Bede.

Heart of the Headland

CONCLUSION

'If we do not want to allow the world to sink into chaos, we must release the love which is trapped in the heart of all humans.' Nikos Kazantzakis.

My narrative centres on St Hilda and her church on Hartlepool Headland. When I set out to write about them I found that there was so much more. The story reaches right back into the beginnings of English Christianity. We are lucky that history has left clues, and we know so much about these pioneers, and we are lucky to have Bede to tell us about their characters, and how they struggled to bring us Christianity and a peaceful country to live in. We are able to look down through the ages at their success rate and perhaps to measure ourselves up against them. There are major questions to ask about how we follow them and what we owe to people who worked so hard to leave us this legacy. They built us churches, as Bede wrote his histories, in the expectation that Christianity would unite us and bring people peaceably together.

Heart of the Headland

This grand old church built on the ridge of hard rock, on a little peninsular in the North Sea holds so many memories and legends. Set on the foundations of earlier churches, right in the middle of the site of St Hilda's first monastery. I could not write just about the architecture or just tell the life of St Hilda. I was drawn into early Christianity history and its champions. How St Hilda's stands intact braving the elements after more than 800 years of history, continuing the tradition set by St Hilda so long ago.

Then the old problem crops up again: that today's congregation is charged with its upkeep, and finding adequate funds to deal with the unstable tower and the cracks in the buttresses, the caving in of the clerestory windows, and the damp in the walls. This old church holds not just the memories and aspirations of its architects and funders through the ages, of course. It is burdened with all the hopes and strivings of the first Anglo-Saxon Christians - the missionaries and their monasteries. It reaches far back into the past to link up with the Iona community, and it is almost true to say it has the personal blessing of St Aidan and the Venerable Bede. Hopefully its significant history helps to carry it into the future, continuing to bring people together, inspiring congregation and visitors and the talented artistic and musical populations that come to it, with the meaning that it carries, long into the future.

Elisabeth Westhead

BIBLIOGRAPHY

The Isle of St Hild. Ed. Bob Beagrie

The Buildings of England. Nikolaus Pevsner

History of Hartlepool. Sir Cuthbert Sharp

The Private Lives of the Saints. Janine Ramirez

Ecclesiastical History of the English People. Bede. Trans Leo Shirley Price

The Age of Bede. Bede. Trans. J.F. Webb

Anglo-Saxon Hartlepool and the Foundations of English Christianity. Robin Daniels

MY THANKS

I have had help and encouragement both from friends and from people I have never met before. I cannot finish without expressing my gratitude to them all.

It was Ian L who said no-one had written a book about our church, encouraged me to write it, and made charcoal sketches of the architecture. There was Leo, with whom I spent many hours discussing Anglo-Saxons, Ashley for her attention to my script. Judy and Kay and Ian P for all their support in various ways. John just put up with me boring him too frequently.

I was amazed and delighted that the Archdeacon of Auckland (that is Auckland in Durham, not Auckland, New Zealand) found the time to write a foreword for the book.

Then I need to thank Paul from the United Reform Church for coming out and taking photos of the stained-glass windows, and Rob from the Oxford Road Baptist Church for giving up his time to scan

Heart of the Headland

my large paper-based images. It was quite special to be receiving help from Hartlepool churches of other denominations.

It has taken me nearly a year to put this book together, from getting the idea and writing it, to collecting the pictures and working with the publishing team.

So last but not least, I must express my gratitude to Stella, Amy and the Production2 team at WMS in Milton Keynes. It is intensive work revising the text and checking for errors. Amy has been very patient and meticulous in interpreting my foibles. She has also drawn a lovely map for me and another WMS artist has interpreted my dreams so beautifully in creating an imaginary sketch of Hilda and Aelfflaed working together in the Headland monastery. Without months of support from them, this book would not be what it is. So many many thanks to Maple Publishing and their studios.

APPENDIX

Detailing: STAINED GLASS WINDOWS, ARCHITECTS and ORGAN

The Stained Glass Windows of St Hilda's Church Hartlepool

SOUTH WALL (Starting at the Chancel)

The boy Jesus by the foreshore. (Boys Brigade Memorial) 1924 Heaton BB

St Hilda of Hartlepool 1914 (unsigned)

The Road to Emmaus. 1880s Clayton and Bell

St George. 1920s (unsigned)

St Bega. 1920s (unsigned)

The Parable of the Talents ('Well done thou good and faithful servant'). 1874 W

The Birth of Jesus. Jesus' preaching ministry. The Crucifixion. 1867. W or WH

Heart of the Headland

The good Samaritan. The Ascension. A woman giving alms (Dorcas?) 1867 W or WH

Abraham and Sarah. Simeon and Anna. John the Evangelist and Dorcas? 1880s Clayton and Bell

King Arthur. Christ on a fishing boat. St Francis. 1926 Horace Wilkinson

NORTH WALL. Starting at the chancel

1) The Light of the World (after Holman Hunt). 1930 Heaton BB

2) The True Vine. 1910 Heaton BB

3) Jesus with children . 1960s influenced by Wailes

4) Faith Hope and Charity. 1891 Heaton, Butler and Bayne

5) St John the Evangelist. The Good Shepherd. St Peter. 1879-95? Heaton BB

6) Christ with a child among the Disciples. Late 1880s Heaton BB

7) The Venerable Bede. Christ,preacher of righteousness. St Aidan 1890-1905. HBB

8) St Hilda. Christ the light of the World. St Cuthbert.1907 Heaton,Butler and Bayne

Elisabeth Westhead

9) Angels around the Virgin and Child. 1910 (unsigned)

HBB. - Heaton Butler and Bayne

CB - Clayton and Bell

W - William Wailes

WH - Ward and Hughes

HW - Horace Wilkinson

EAST WINDOW. Top to Bottom - Left to right

X - The road to Emmaus. Jesus and 2 companions. Jesus is holding a censer.

1a The Entry into Jerusalem (Luke 19)

1b The road to Calvary (Luke 23)

1c The baptism of Jesus. (Matthew 3)

2a The Flight to Egypt (Matthew 2)

2b The Adoration of the Magi (Matthew 2)

2c The Holy Family at work (sewing and carpentry)

2d The Resurrection

Heart of the Headland

2e Christ and Mary Magdalen

3a The risen Christ greets Mary Magdalen (John 20)

3b Jesus Crucified

3c The women at the Tomb

3d The Ascension

3e The Last Supper

4a Christ in Majesty

4b The Shepherds and the Angels (Luke 2)

4c. ....?

Architect- Pritchard. Stained-Glass - Clayton and Bell

ARCHITECTS OF THE RESTORATION PROJECTS

Pevsner: County Durham P.30 The nave of the church was restored in 1865 by **Charles Hodgson Fowler** (all the roofs are his). He was the son of a Nottinghamshire vicar who trained in London with Sir Gilbert Scott, the most prolific of the leading 19th century architects. In the mid 1820s he established himself in Durham and became the consultant architect to the cathedrals of Durham, York, Lincoln and Rochester. He worked on St Hilda's Church at the age of 25.

Elisabeth Westhead

J.P.Pritchett of Darlington built a new chancel in 1869, but it was shorter than the original medieval chancel had been.

Douglas Caroe was brought up in Liverpool, where his Danish father ran a large flour mill, and he studied at Trinity College, Cambridge, and then trained with J.L.Pearson, perhaps the greatest of the late Victorian architects. He set up practice in London, becoming increasingly interested in ecclesiastical work. He succeeded Hodgson Fowler as architect to Durham Cathedral, and became Consulting Architect to the Ecclesiastical Commission, Canterbury Cathedral, Westminster Abbey, etc.

Because the 1869 chancel was shorter than the mediaeval original, in 1916, W.D.Caroe drew up plans to the full dimension of the mediaeval structure. A Restoration Committee was formed in 1924, but it was 1927 before William Grey, the shipbuilder, made a major gift to enable the plan to be finalised. The original design for the East End window by Pritchett (Glass by Clayton and Bell) was designed for 3 lancets at the East End. Caroe's East End had four larger lancets, but it was decided to use the 1869 glass. The lower parts of the window are filled with the 1869 glass, though some of the architectural surrounds have been removed. The rest of each window has plain glass. It is good that the high quality Clayton and Bell glass was retained, albeit arranged somewhat haphazardly. It may however, give the impression that the upper part of the window had been damaged. See above for list of scenes covered.

MAKERS OF THE STAINED GLASS WINDOWS

Clayton and Bell established their partnership in 1856. They had met in the offices of Sir Gilbert Scott, where Clayton was an experienced designer and artist, whom Scott had met when he became involved in the completion of the Palace of Westminster following the early death of Pugin. Bell was an apprentice and trained as an architect, but Scott recognised his talent as an artist and encouraged the two men to set up their own business. Scott gave numerous important commissions to them and they were also the favoured stained-glass designers for major architects such as Pearson and Street. Within only a handful of years they had become the largest and most successful stained-glass firm in the country. They used high quality glass and, despite the size of their workforce in the factory, careful standards of design were always maintained. The volume of their work reduced dramatically after the First World War, when stained-glass quickly ceased to be the favoured medium for memorials, and the firm became almost a one-man band after the workshop was bombed out in the Blitz. The last Bell closed the firm in 1993.

The first window, to the right, The Young Christ, commemorates the setting up of the Boys Brigade. 1924. The boy's face is a portrait of one of the existing members of the BB. The background shows features of the Headland beach. It is unsigned, but undoubtedly by Heaton, Butler and Bayne. The firm was established in London in 1855 and for a few years their remarkable use of a wide range of colours made them one of the most innovative stained-glass firms in the country. By 1870 their style became more mainstream but their high quality remained. By the turn of the century, their style had become rather heavier and more sentimental but the quality of manufacture remained high. After the First World War, their output became much smaller and the artistic quality began to suffer until the firm fizzled out in the late 1930s, a sad shadow of the great days.

Chancel, south aisle, south-west: the Parable of the Talents. Date commemorated 1874. Unsigned but probably by Wailes. In the bright, rather hot colours that were by then beginning to go out of favour. William Wailes was the major force behind the re-establishment of Neo-Gothic stained-glass design and manufacture, and was used by Pugin for some years. Wailes set up in business in Newcastle in 1838

Heart of the Headland

and soon became the leading and largest stained-glass firm, employing some 200 people. He succumbed to the competition from the likes of C & B and HB & B, and the firm gradually dwindled for many years, until (long after Wailes's own death) it closed early in the 20th century. His early designs were carefully based on mediaeval precedent and he used bright , strong colours that became more muted from the 1860s as the designs became more formulaic and stilted.

Nave, south aisle, south-west. King Arthur, Christ aboard a fishing boat, St Francis, dated 1926. Signed by Horace Wilkinson. Wilkinson trained in the 1880s and 1890s with several of the large London studios and set up his own firm at the turn of the century, already approaching 40 years of age. He continued until he was over 80 when he was succeeded by his son Arthur. His work was almost always of the highest quality of design and execution, with carefully delineated figures and a wide palette of colours. He was much admired by Caroe and there are Wilkinson windows in many of Caroe's churches, (as here). This is perhaps the best window in the church from the point of view of manufacture and colour.

From notes by Colin Menzies. July 2014.

Elisabeth Westhead

ORGAN

The organ was built in 1871 by Peter Conacher of Huddersfield with entirely mechanical action. It was re-built by Wood and Wordsworth (Leeds) in the 1930s, with pneumatic action. It was again re-built with electric action in 1990 by Adrian Cook of Stockton-on-Tees, when some tonal additions were made electronically.

Peter Conacher had trained in his native Edinburgh, then gone to work for two or three years in Germany. He returned to Edinburgh and founded his own business, which failed after only three years , as the Church of Scotland maintained its ban on organs. He moved to London and worked with William Hill, perhaps the greatest of the British builders, quickly becoming a senior foreman. Some years later he was sent to Huddersfield to supervise the erection and finishing of a large new Hill organ and he sensed that Yorkshire's increasing prosperity and population represented a major new market. The following year he resigned his position with Hill and established his own business, Peter Conacher and Co., His organs were of the best and the original instrument here at St Hilda's would have been beautifully built with a bright and bold tone.

Heart of the Headland

When it was rebuilt in 1930 by Wood Wordsworth of Leeds with tubular pneumatic action. Their work was not as good, though the key action would be considerably lighter than the mechanical original and was still reasonably operational by the 1980s. Surprisingly, although the effective size of the church was increased by the Caroe restoration, no tonal changes seem to have been made.

Rebuilt in 1990 by Adrian Cooke of Stockton-on-Tees with a new console and direct electric action and some additional electronic ranks, intended not to compromise the pipe organ. In 2011, the electronic ranks were replaced with new samples taken from contemporary instruments, using the Hauptwerk system. 49 speaking stops (of which 21 are electronic).

Colin Menzies. July 2014. Organ notes edited. I.L.P. Feb 2025.

www.ingramcontent.com/pod-product-compliance
Lightning Source LLC
Chambersburg PA
CBHW051419070526
44584CB00023B/3491